ALASKAN INUITS

HISTORY, CULTURE AND LIFESTYLE
INUITS FOR KIDS BOOK

3RD GRADE SOCIAL STUDIES

BABY PROFESSOR
EDUCATION KIDS

Speedy Publishing LLC
40 E. Main St. #1156
Newark, DE 19711
www.speedypublishing.com
Copyright 2017

In this book, we're going to talk all about the Alaskan Inuits. So, let's get right to it!

WHO ARE THE INUIT PEOPLE?

The Inuit people have lived in the cold tundra for thousands of years. They originally settled along the coast of Alaska, but eventually their populations spread out to other regions surrounding the Arctic Circle. Today, descendants of these native people still live in the harsh conditions of the Arctic tundra.

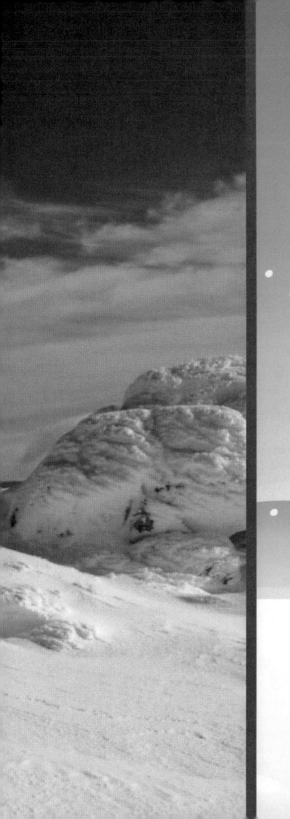

This large geographic coastal area includes sections of northern Canada, the state of Alaska, the Russian region called Siberia, and the country of Greenland. Some of the different groups of people in these areas share common ancestors and others don't. However, they have similar lifestyles that enable them to survive in the Arctic.

HOW DID THE INUIT SURVIVE IN SUCH HARSH CONDITIONS?

There is almost no vegetation on the tundra, so in order to survive the Inuit depended on hunting and fishing. They hunted for large land mammals, such as polar bears and caribou, as well as marine mammals, such as seals and whales.

SEALS

They built harpoons, which are a type of spear, to hunt and kill these large animals. They created the first kayak boats and used them to hunt marine mammals and catch fish. Because their food had a high fat content, it sustained them with long-term energy during the coldest months of the year.

HOW DID THE INUIT PEOPLE HUNT WHALES?

Inuit hunters had to work together in order to hunt and kill a large whale. Twenty or more hunters would travel together on a huge boat. They each carried a harpoon. They took the skins of seals and made balloons with them, which they filled up with air to make them buoyant.

When they spotted a whale, they speared it, but because they had attached the buoyant seal skin balloons, the whale was unable to dive down under the water to escape. Each time the whale arose to the surface, they would harpoon it again until it couldn't fight any longer. Then, the hunters would secure it to the boat and bring it back to shore.

It took a great deal of work to take down a whale, but the Inuit didn't waste one bit of the whale because they had great respect for the giant mammal.

One whale would be enough meat to feed a small community for a full year. In addition to the meat, they used the whale's skin, its oil, its bones, and its blubber.

HOW DID THE INUIT PEOPLE GET FROM PLACE TO PLACE?

The Inuit used dogsleds to travel long distances over land. Over time, they domesticated wolves and they evolved into husky dogs.

These dogs had the strength and stamina to pull the sleds that were largely constructed from whalebones. Since there were few landmarks, they frequently used piled stones in the shape of a person to mark specific locations for reference. These piled stones were named "inuksuk." Over time, the inuksuk became a symbol of friendship among peoples.

For traveling over the water, the Inuits used kayaks for one or two people. They also constructed larger umiaqs, which were huge boats for transporting people, sled dogs, and supplies.

WHAT KIND OF HOMES DID THEY LIVE IN?

In ancient times, people frequently used wood and mud to construct homes. The Inuit people didn't have these resources in the Arctic. However, the Inuit still found ways to make homes they could live in. During the months of the summer, they took driftwood or the bones from whales to create a structure.

Then they stretched the skins of animals over the frames they created to make a dwelling. During the winter, they used compressed snow to construct circular structures called igloos. Even though these homes were constructed from cold materials, the heat generated on the inside from body heat and other sources kept the temperature inside warmer than the outside.

IGLOO

WHAT KIND OF CLOTHING DID THEY WEAR?

To stay alive in the harsh tundra, the Inuit created very warm clothing for themselves. They used animal pelts and furs to create their clothes, such as pants and shirts. They created large jackets known as "anoraks" from the skins of seals and caribou.

They also further insulated their clothing with fur from animals, such as rabbits or foxes. They sometimes even used the fur from polar bears. They also wore insulated mukluks, which were soft boots made from animal skins.

INUIT FAMILIES

Although the men and women didn't have formal vows of matrimony or a wedding ceremony, they still lived together as husbands and wives. The husbands were the hunters and fishermen. Their wives raised the children and also sewed the clothes and prepared the meals.

INUIT CUSTOMS AND CULTURE

The Inuit had a huge amount of respect for the animals that sustained them.

During the hunt, they had certain rituals and traditions that they followed. They often performed songs that paid homage to the spirits of the animals they had killed.

Many of their myths are inspired by the snowy regions in which they live. They felt that the aurora borealis, which is a display of color lights caused by solar storms, was magical and it became a part of many of their myths.

The dark night sky as well as the long winters and freezing Arctic Ocean became the backdrop for many legends told by oral storytelling.

INUIT MYTHS

The Inuit people in different regions have
told these stories for many generations.

THE MYTH OF THE SUN AND THE MOON

The goddess of the sun was called Malina and her brother Anningan was the god of the moon. They lived in the same house but they fought with each other all the time. One day, Malina got very angry at Anningan and she spread black tar all over his face. Then, because she was afraid he would be vengeful and come after her, she began to run through the heavens.

This is how she became the sun. Of course, her brother began to chase after her and this is how he became the moon. Sometimes Anningan was so determined to catch his sister that he forgot to eat and became thinner and thinner, which explains the moon's phases. Once a month, for a span of three days, he paused to eat and that is when he disappeared from the sky.

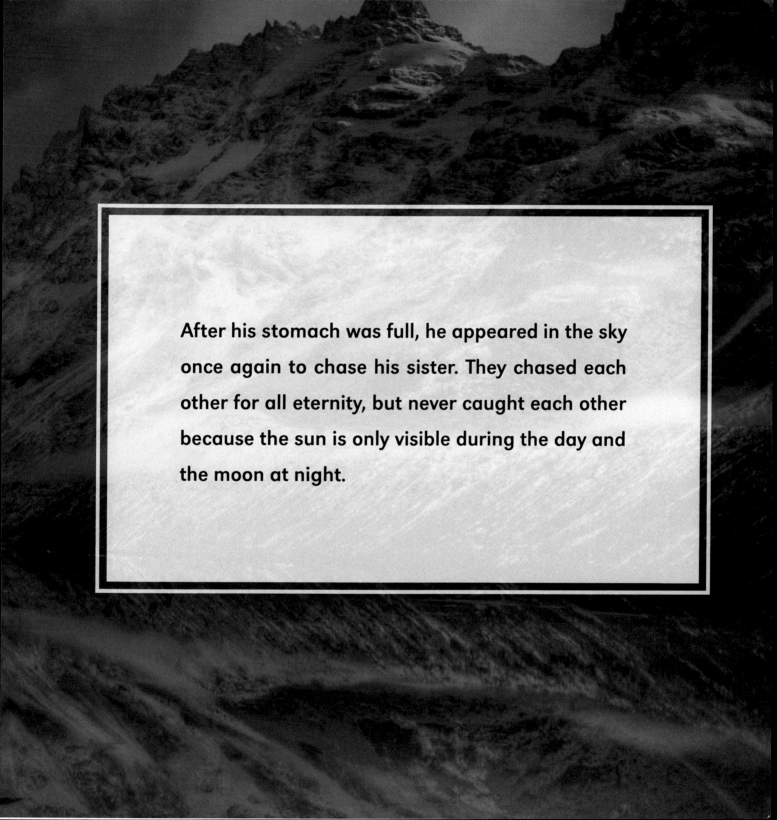

After his stomach was full, he appeared in the sky once again to chase his sister. They chased each other for all eternity, but never caught each other because the sun is only visible during the day and the moon at night.

THE SPIRIT OF THE SEA

Sedna was a stubborn young girl. She had many suitors who wanted to marry her, but she refused all of them. Her father was annoyed with her stubbornness so he married her off to a wild dog. He regretted his decision later and decided to drown her dog husband so that Sedna would be free again. After this happened, Sedna and her children were starving because they couldn't support themselves so Sedna gave up her children and returned home to her parents.

One day a seabird showed up at her house. He was disguised as a young man and he asked Sedna to marry him. She left her parents' home and went away to live with him. However, she soon discovered that he was not a man at all, but a fulmar, which is a tubenosed seabird.

Sedna's father came to visit her, but when he saw she was married to a bird, he pleaded with her to return home with him.

As they were traveling away over the water, her bird husband began to create a horrible winter storm.

Sedna's father was fearful and decided he needed to return Sedna to her husband so he began to throw her off the boat. Sedna grasped the edge of the boat tightly and her father was terrified that he would die so he cut off her fingers. Sedna died at the bottom of the sea and all the sea creatures evolved from her fingers.

In 2003, a large planetoid was discovered on the cold outer edges of our solar system and astronomers named it Sedna in honor of the Inuit sea spirit.

SEDNA

INUIT COUPLE

HOW DO THE INUIT PEOPLE LIVE TODAY?

Before World War II, the Inuit people had little contact with the rest of the world. Their world was harsh but they had it all to themselves. Once in a while Europeans passed through and they often brought diseases that had a devastating impact on the native people. When the war was over, the "Cold War" between the United States and Russia began.

Now with easy access to airplanes, the two superpowers were in close proximity in the Arctic, which meant permanent settlements around airbases and radar stations.

The Inuit population got larger due to the better health care that was available, but they were sometimes forced to abandon their traditional lifestyle and some were required to move to cities by 1960.

A HARDY PEOPLE

The Inuit people have lived in the harsh Arctic tundra for thousands of years. They have hunted the land mammals and marine mammals with harpoons to survive. They have domesticated wolves into husky dogs to pull their sleds across the snow. Their myths and legends tell stories of the snowy environment they live in.

Awesome! Now that you've read about the Alaskan Inuits you may want to read facts about Native American tribes in the Baby Professor book The 10 Largest Native American Tribes.